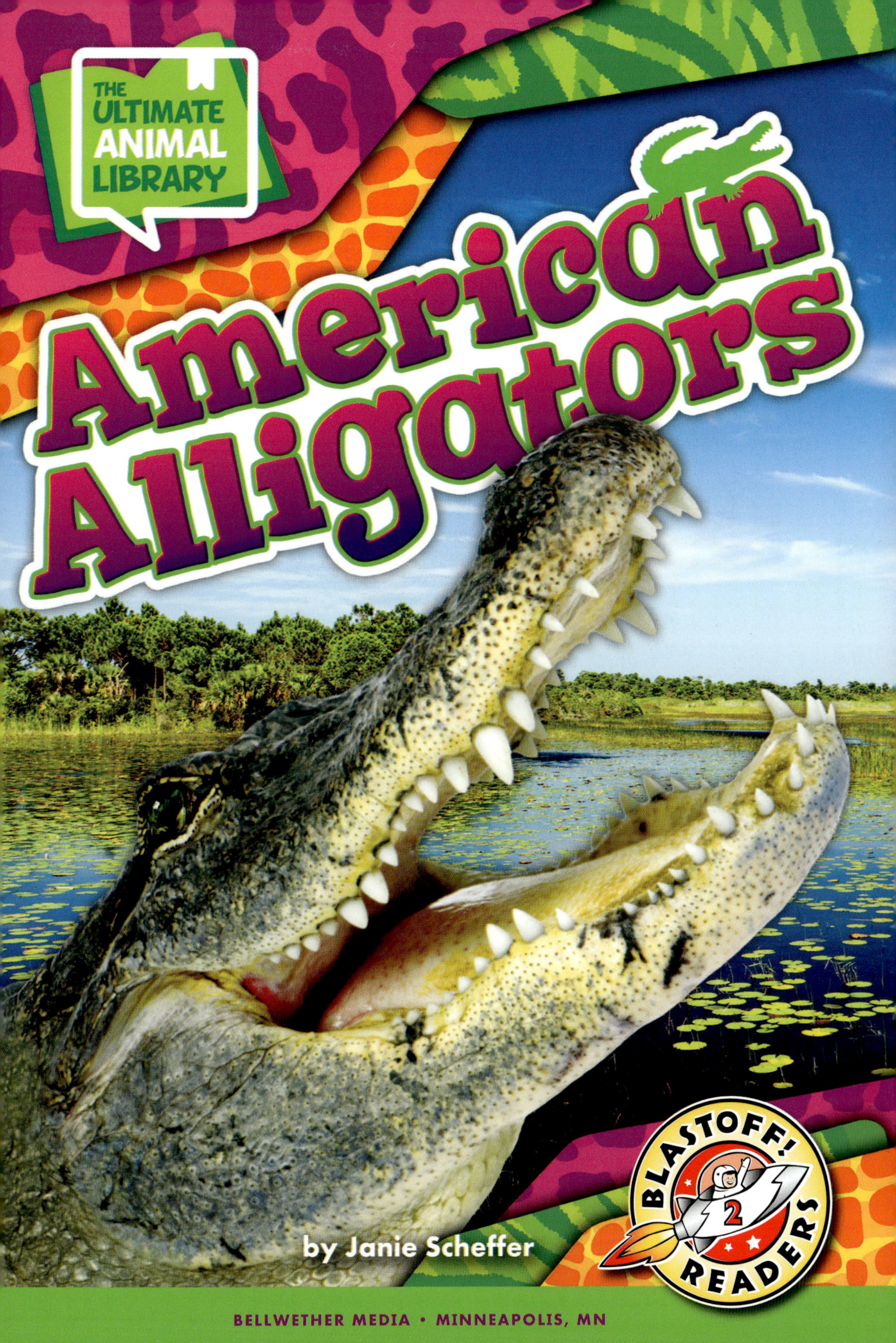
THE ULTIMATE ANIMAL LIBRARY
American Alligators
by Janie Scheffer
BLASTOFF! 2 READERS
BELLWETHER MEDIA • MINNEAPOLIS, MN

Blastoff! Readers are carefully developed by literacy experts to build reading stamina and move students toward fluency by combining standards-based content with developmentally appropriate text.

LEVELS

Level 1 provides the most support through repetition of high-frequency words, light text, predictable sentence patterns, and strong visual support.

Level 2 offers early readers a bit more challenge through varied sentences, increased text load, and text-supportive special features.

Level 3 advances early-fluent readers toward fluency through increased text load, less reliance on photos, advancing concepts, longer sentences, and more complex special features.

★ **Blastoff! Universe**

Reading Level

Grade K

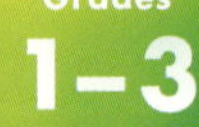

Grades 1–3

Grade 4

This edition first published in 2025 by Bellwether Media, Inc.

Library of Congress Cataloging-in-Publication Data

LC record for American Alligators available at: https://lccn.loc.gov/2024012091

Editor: Elizabeth Neuenfeldt Series Designer: Veah Demmin

Printed in the United States of America, North Mankato, MN.

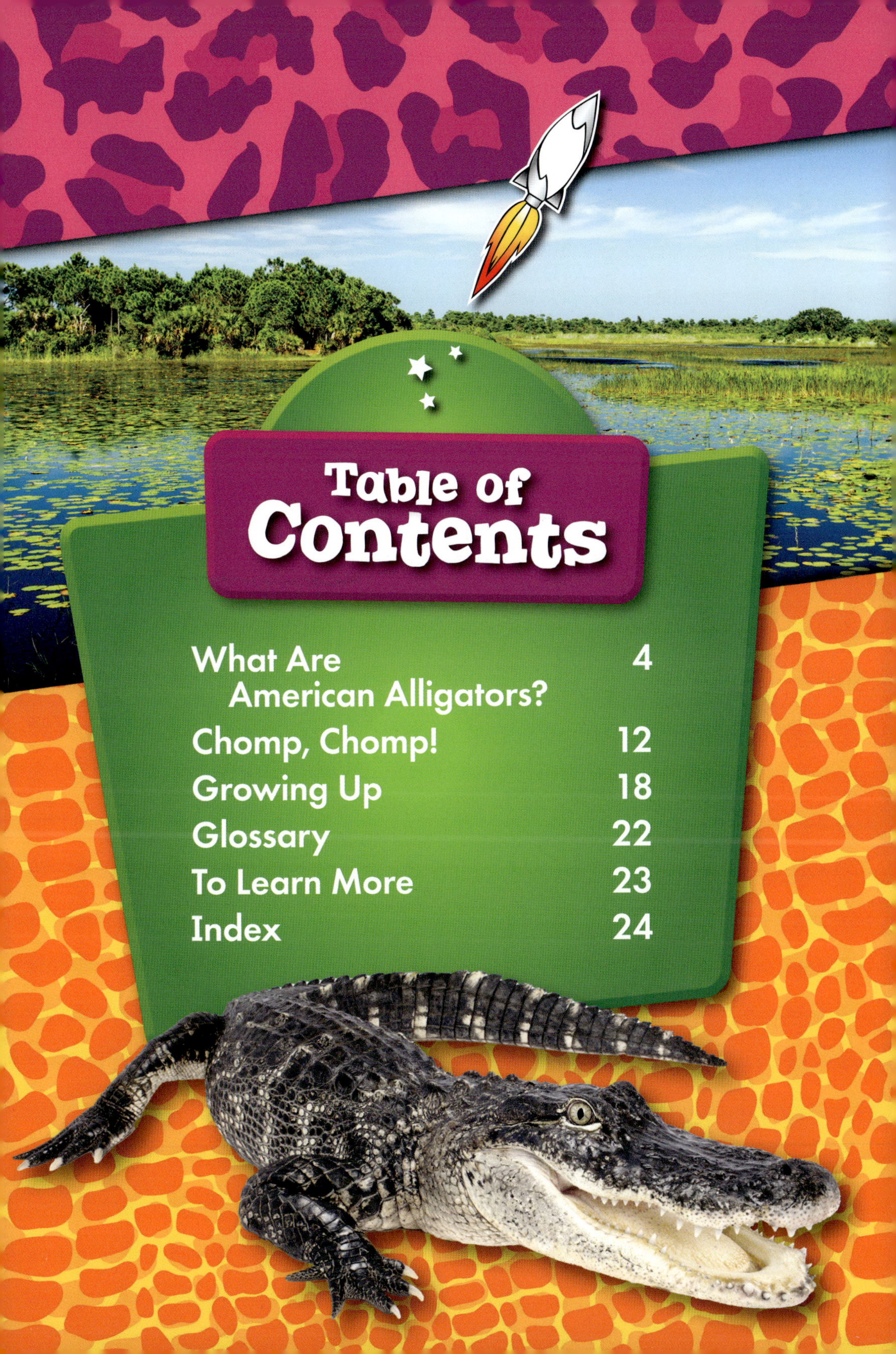

Table of Contents

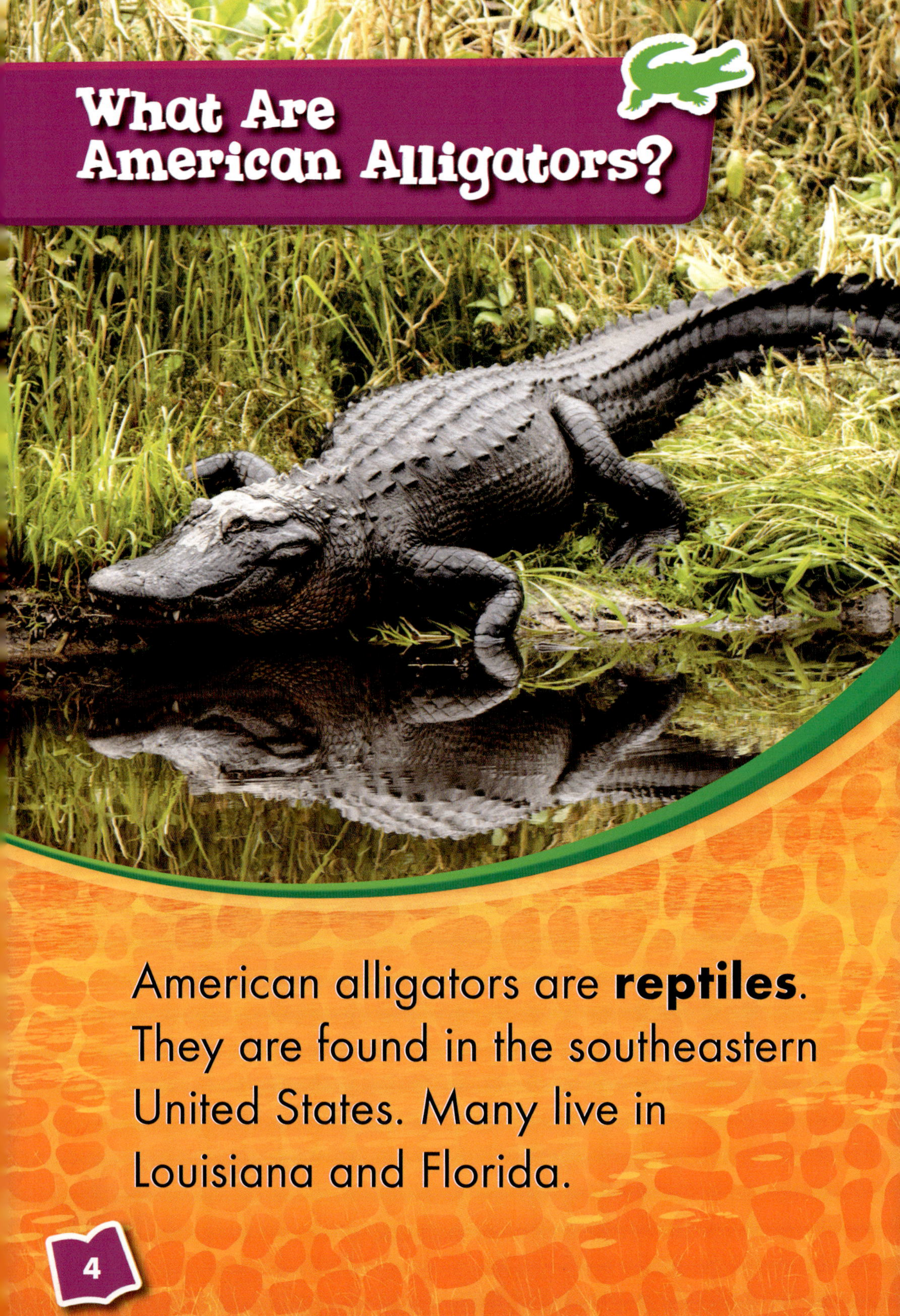

What Are American Alligators?

American alligators are **reptiles**. They are found in the southeastern United States. Many live in Louisiana and Florida.

American Alligator Report

Range

Status in the Wild

Habitats

lakes

rivers

swamps

These alligators are long! Males can be 10 to 15 feet (3 to 4.6 meters) long.

Some males can weigh 1,000 pounds (454 kilograms). Females are smaller.

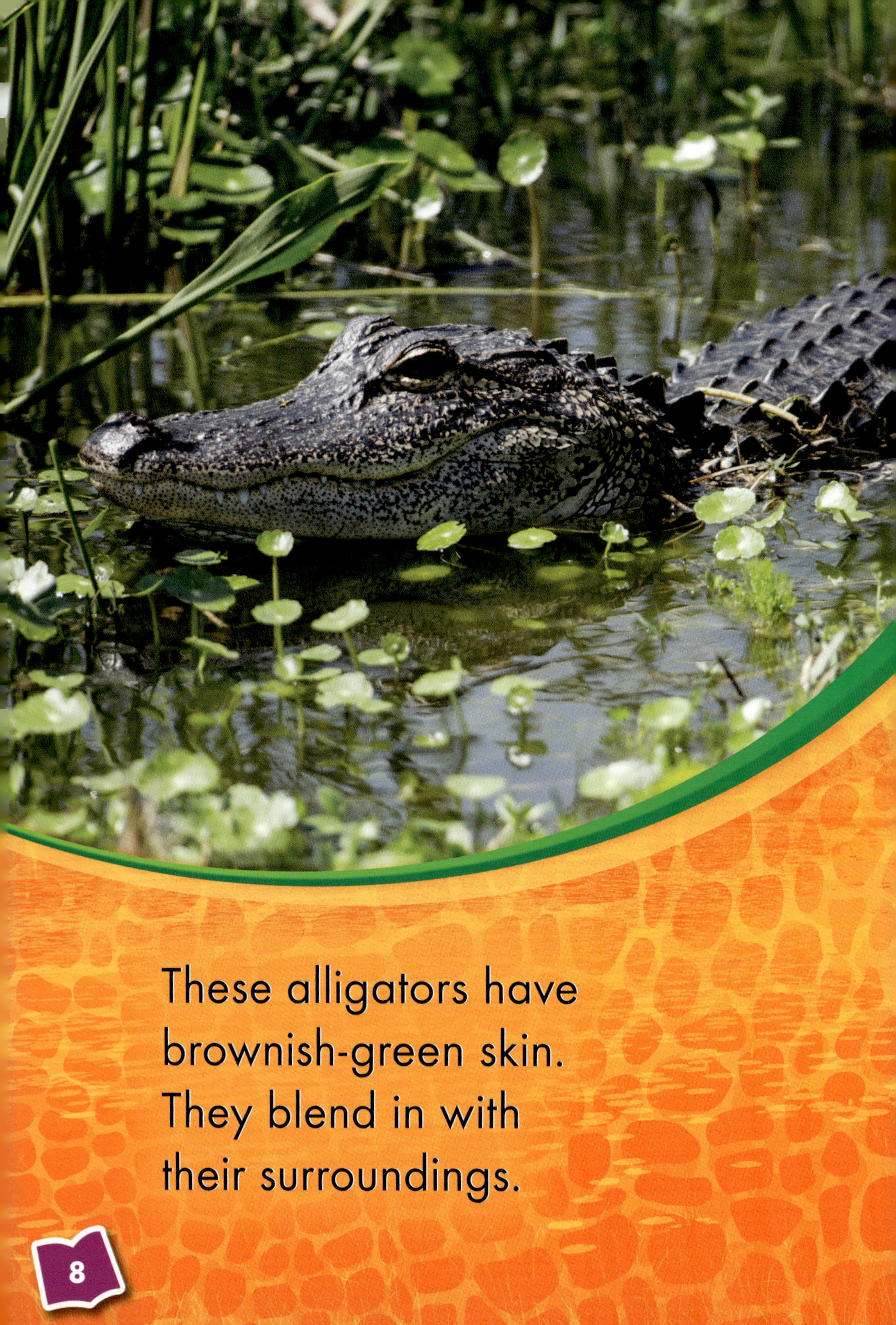

These alligators have brownish-green skin. They blend in with their surroundings.

Their backs are covered with **scutes**. These keep alligators safe from harm.

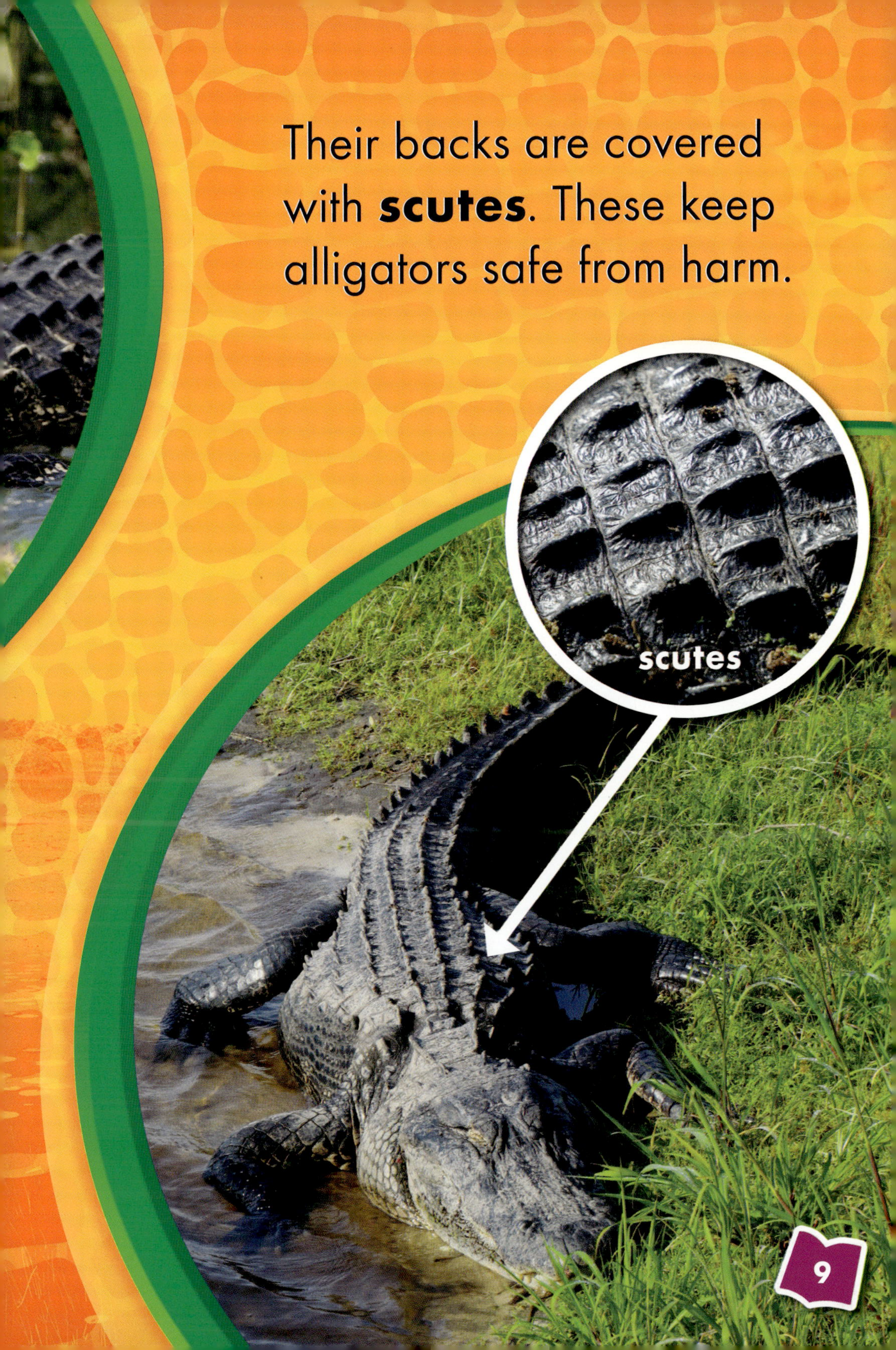

These alligators have long, rounded **snouts**. Their teeth are sharp. They have a powerful bite!

They have **webbed feet** and long, strong tails. These help alligators swim.

webbed foot

Spot an American Alligator

long snout

scutes

long, strong tail

snout

Chomp, Chomp!

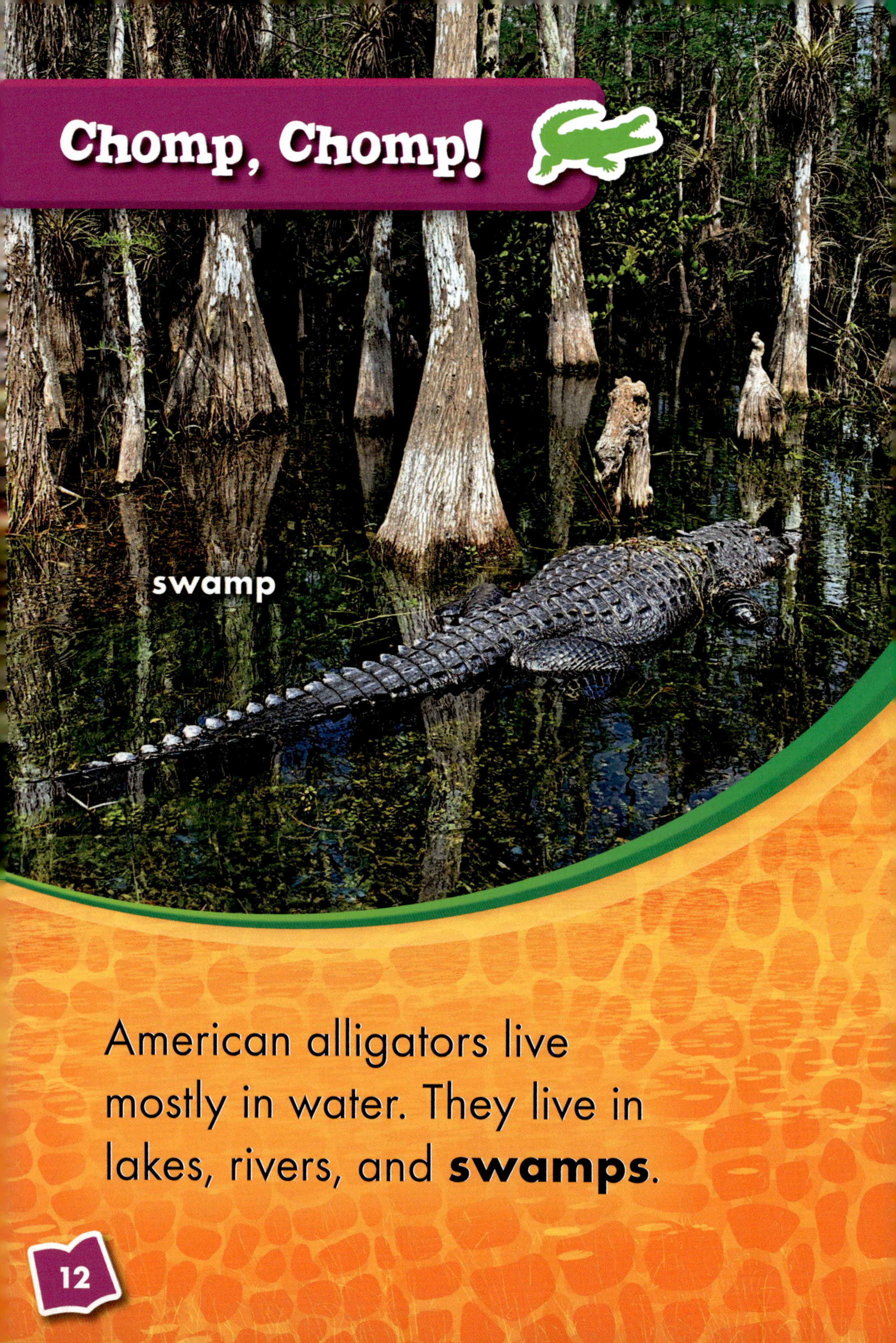

American alligators live mostly in water. They live in lakes, rivers, and **swamps**.

Some live in small groups.

These alligators lay
in the sun to stay warm.

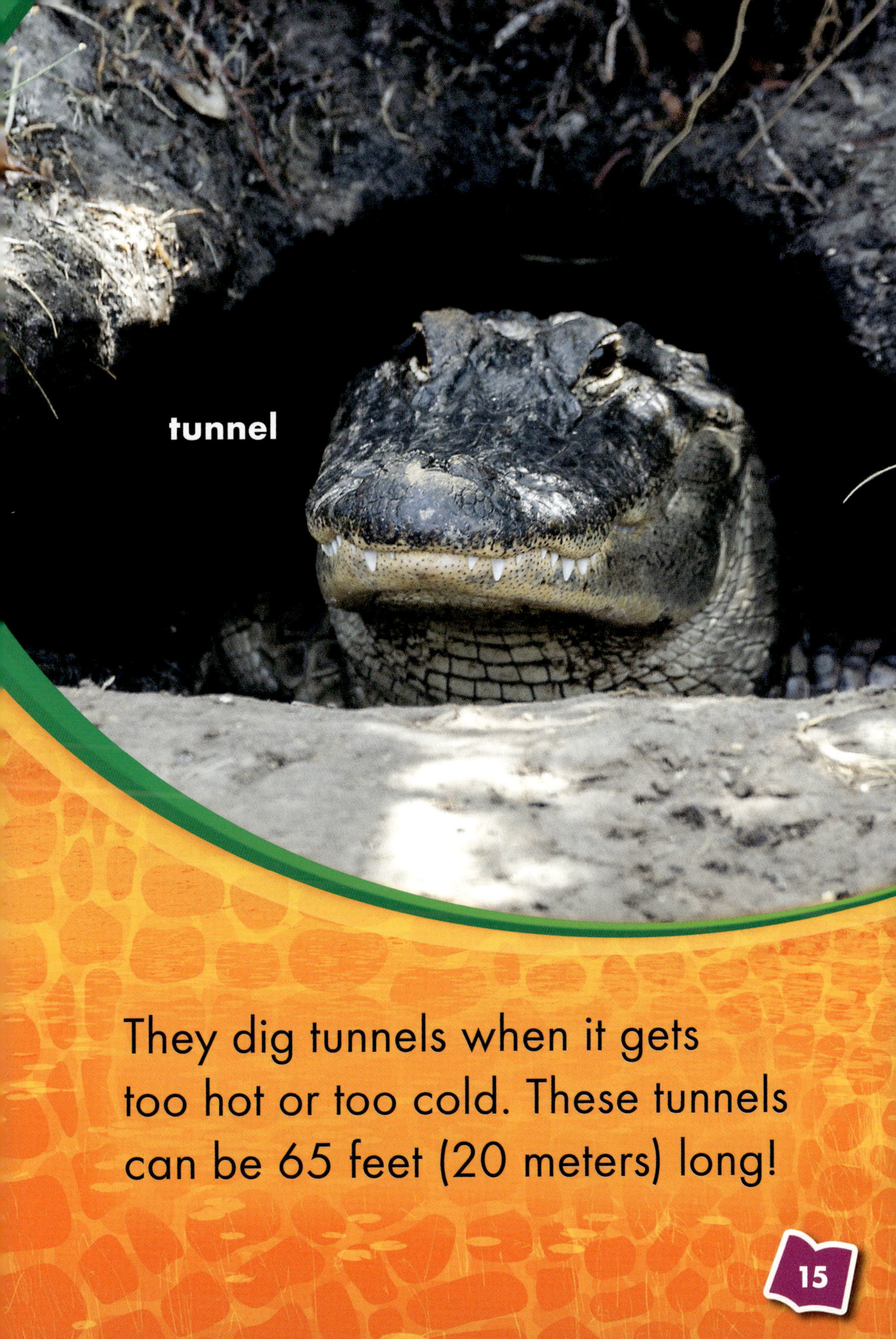

They dig tunnels when it gets too hot or too cold. These tunnels can be 65 feet (20 meters) long!

These alligators are **carnivores**. They eat birds, fish, and reptiles.

They mostly hunt at night. They catch **prey** with their sharp teeth and strong jaws.

Growing Up

American alligators build nests on land. Females lay up to 90 eggs!

Hatchlings make noise when they are ready to **hatch**. They are black with yellow stripes.

eggs

hatchlings

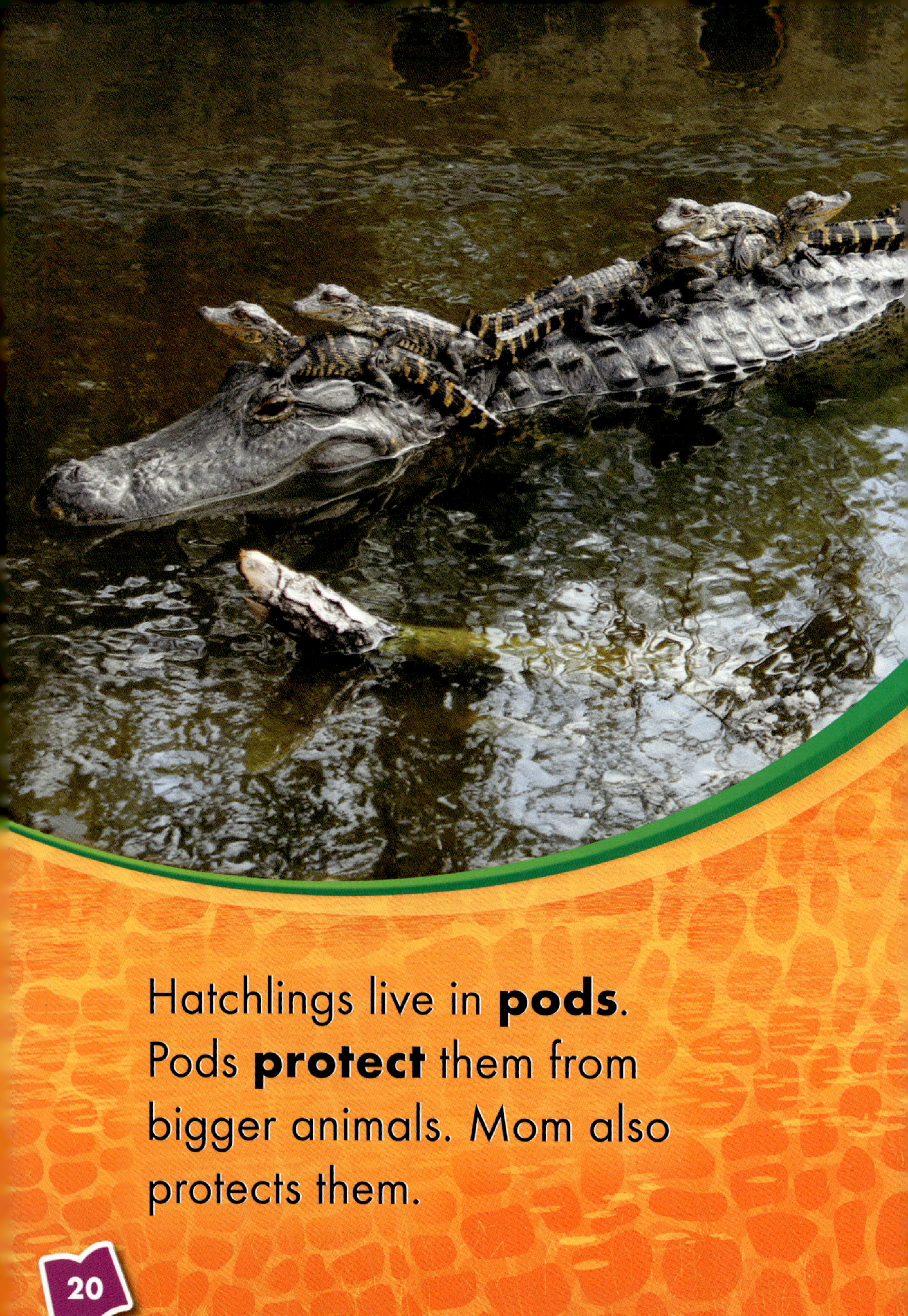

Hatchlings live in **pods**. Pods **protect** them from bigger animals. Mom also protects them.

In about two years, American alligators can live on their own!

Life of an American Alligator

Name of Babies

hatchlings

Number of Eggs

up to 90

Time Spent with Mom

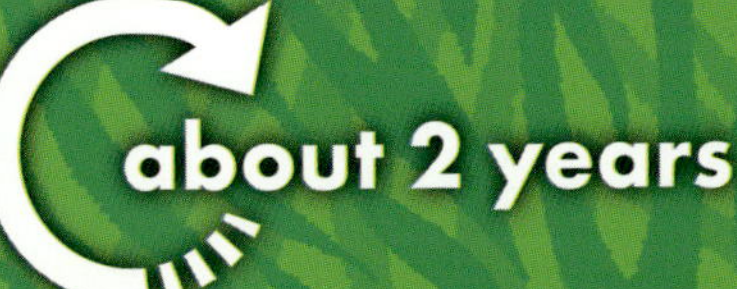

Life Span

Glossary

carnivores—animals that only eat meat

hatch—to break out of an egg

hatchlings—baby American alligators

pods—small groups of young American alligators

prey—animals that are hunted by other animals for food

protect—to keep safe

reptiles—cold-blooded animals that have backbones and lay eggs

scutes—bony plates or scales that cover the bodies of some animals

snouts—the noses and mouths of some animals

swamps—wetlands filled with trees and other woody plants

webbed feet—feet with thin skin that connects the toes

To Learn More

AT THE LIBRARY

Feldman, Thea. *Alligators and Crocodiles Can't Chew!: And Other Amazing Facts*. New York, N.Y.: Simon Spotlight, 2021.

Grack, Rachel. *Alligators*. Minneapolis, Minn.: Bellwether Media, 2020.

Shields, Jennifer. *Alligator or Crocodile? A Compare and Contrast Book*. Mt. Pleasant, S.C.: Arbordale Publishing, 2023.

ON THE WEB

FACTSURFER

Factsurfer.com gives you a safe, fun way to find more information.

1. Go to www.factsurfer.com.
2. Enter "American alligators" into the search box and click 🔍.
3. Select your book cover to see a list of related content.

Index

The images in this book are reproduced through the courtesy of: InnaPoka, series patterns; Eric Isselee, cover (American alligator), pp. 11, 23; Fotoluminate LLC, cover background, interior background; Bahruz Rzayev, cover (alligator icon); reptiles4all, p. 3; SunflowerMomma, p. 4; deannalindsey, p. 6; Joe Blossom/ Alamy, p. 7; Dennis W Donohue, p. 8; Laurel A Egan, p. 9; Danita Delimont, pp. 9 (inset), 10 (inset), 13; RICIfoto, pp. 10-11; jaimie tuchman, p. 12; Luis Saint Amant, p. 14; 6381380, p. 15; Svetlana Foote, pp. 16-17; Heiko Kiera, p. 17 (alligator); slowmotiongli, p. 17 (birds); M-Production, p. 17 (fish); Korkin Vadim, p. 17 (reptiles); George Shelley/ Getty, p. 18 (inset); mark stephens photography, pp. 18-19; Marc Pletcher, p. 20; Will E. Davis, p. 21.